Usborne Talk and Count
HOW MANY
MONSTERS?

Heather Amery
Illustrated by Malcolm Livingstone

Consultant: Betty Root
Centre for the Teaching of Reading
University of Reading

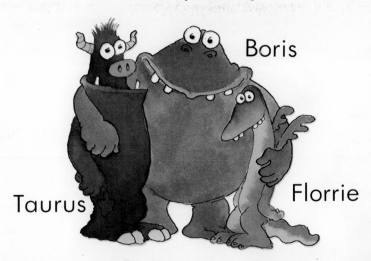

Boris

Florrie

Taurus

The monsters are going for a picnic.
Boris is making the sandwiches.

Florrie has been shopping.
What is Taurus doing?

The monsters have started off down the road.
How are they traveling to their picnic?

Who has the picnic baskets?
How many monsters can you see?

What has happened to poor Boris?
What other animals can you see?

What will happen to Florrie.
How many monsters?

Poor Boris has to leave his car.
How do they all cross the river?

How many ducks are there?
How many monsters can you see?

What are Boris and Florrie doing?
Why is Taurus in trouble?

What other animals can you see?
How many of them are monsters?

The monster band marches down the street.
What are Boris, Taurus and Florrie doing?

Where are the picnic baskets?
How many monsters can you count?

Boris, Taurus and Florrie reach the beach.
What are they doing now?

How many birds are flying?
How many monsters can you see?

It is time for the picnic.
How many monsters now?

First published in 1985
Usborne Publishing Ltd
20 Garrick St, London
WC2 9BJ, England
© Usborne Publishing Ltd 1985

The name of Usborne and the device 🐝 are Trade Marks of Usborne Publishing Ltd.

Printed in Portugal